Birth of a Daughter

Birth of a Daughter

Poems by

Samantha Kolber

Cover design by Shay Culligan
Cover art by Saskia Pyatak, age three

ISBN: 978-1-952326-36-3

Kelsay Books
502 South 1040 East, A-119
American Fork, Utah, 84003

for my daughter, Saskia

Acknowledgments

PoemCity 2019: "A(u)reola"

Root & Rise Quarterly: "What Nourishes Me: Poem at Ten Weeks Pregnant"

Tupelopress.com: "Birth of a Daughter," "The Girl is Three," "What Feral Means to a Writing Mom," and "7-Minute Fairytale"

Many thanks to: my first reader and husband Christopher Pyatak; my other first reader and writer-wife Sarah Cannon; Kirstin Miles, Anthony Immergluck, and the poets from the June 2019 Tupelo 30/30 Project; Geof Hewitt, who taught me the 7-minute writing exercise, which I employed to write "7-Minute Fairytale" (and a plethora of poems over my writing career); Laure-Anne Bosselaar and the Solstice MFA Program at Pine Manor College; Rick Agran; Lizzy Fox; Megan Buchanan; Teresa LaMendola Kabat-Zinn; Stephen McArthur; Kerrin McCadden; Michelle Singer; Turtle Island Children's Center; my Bear Pond Books family; and, of course, Karen Kelsay and the staff at Kelsay Books, who have all midwifed, in one form or another, the birth of this book.

Contents

Cradle the Mother   11

What Nourishes Me: Poem at Ten Weeks Pregnant   12

I Am Marked   17

False Labor at 26 Weeks   18

Feel the Fibroid   21

The Missing Poem: Birth   23

Breastfeeding Dyad   25

A(u)reola   26

Birth of a Daughter   27

Write Like a Fighter   28

My Toddler's Scrambled Eggs   30

Heart Healthy   31

The Girl is Three   33

What Feral Means to a Writing Mom   34

7-Minute Fairytale   35

How to Celebrate a Dead Mom's Birthday   36

To My Daughter Sleeping Soundly in the Middle
of the Night   37

Cradle the Mother

feel the heartbeat
inside heart beat

feel the hand
making its own music

inside the cradle
plates shifting

not forming mountains
but humans

a girl this time
a mother for herself

What Nourishes Me: Poem at Ten Weeks Pregnant

I am awake
at 4:30 am.
I wake all night
to pee and nibble
on crackers. Each
day at this
early morning time—
before sunrise and
the din of neighbors,
before clanging
garbage trucks
and my husband's
alarm—I am
clearly awake
with no purpose yet
though I suspect
my body is preparing me
for those soon-to-come
early morning feedings.

My pregnancy app
tells me only 205
days to go. Great.
Having just endured
six weeks of unending
nausea—the "morning"
sickness that lasts
all day and night,
I'm ready for this
pregnancy to go as
quickly as possible.

I was good in
the very beginning
when the glow of
the plus sign on
the stick wrapped us
in secret grins and
lovemaking. That
magical feeling.
I took daily walks
in the crisp fall air.
I took vitamins
and ate two
eggs each morning.
Then, abruptly, everything
changed. Waves of nausea
carried me through
my days. The smell
of food cooking made
me gag. The taste of
cooked food made me
gag. Headaches, fast
and furious, made me
lie down at 5:00, as
soon as I got home
from work, the sky dark
with winter's arrival.
I stopped walking.
I stopped taking
my vitamins—
which also
made me gag. I
stopped eating eggs
in the morning and

cooked foods altogether.
I started nibbling
like a little mouse
on benign things:
crackers and bananas
and rice cakes. The only
protein-like foods
I wanted were
yogurts and cheeses
and deli meats (I know).
I began going
to bed at 7:30 every
night, bloated and
constipated, nauseous
and headachy. I started
sleeping on a wedge of
two pillows. I had
no idea it would be
this bad, so unlike
my first pregnancy
over a decade ago.

My husband adjusted to
this new normal—he
started making all
the dinners, the lunch
each morning for my son.
He took on cleaning
and food shopping
and so many chores.
He slept on the couch
so as not to disturb
me when he came

to bed late or woke
up early. Little
did he know
my sleep was already
disturbed, like now.

Another thing that
stopped: having sex.
This I miss
the most. More
than coffee and
cooked food and the
yoga class I gave up on,
I miss his skin
on my skin. I miss
his beautiful hairy body
and the fitted puzzle piece
we make together.

In this tenth week, I've
started to feel a little better.
A few acupuncture sessions
and waiting it out, we're
back to sleeping
in the same bed.
In the middle of the night
when I wake to tend
to one of my bodily needs,
sometimes, I lay my hand
on his bare skin—his arm,
his shoulder, his chest,
his belly. He's ticklish
though, and always grabs

my hand, even when he
snores deeply. But I
want his skin. All of it.
More than just my hand
like a sleeping shadow
on his peaceful form,
I want to press every
pore of mine
against him. I want
to suffocate my
body with the feel
of his bare skin
pressing down
on mine. It's that
feeling—that warmth
and total contact—I need.
This is what nourishes me:
his skin touching mine,
filling in
the little voids
of my porous self.

I Am Marked

I am marked, the body does not lie.
Flesh swells and mounds and projects
what it cannot hide. I am a double
entity, like the bearded lady. People stare
as I waddle down the street, but they don't see me.

I am marked. Growing cells and tissues inside
to form the new brain in the soft skull, the new
femurs, tibiae, fingers and toes—a two-and-a-half pound
replica, my swollen belly unwieldy
as a fat furuncle. I am just this extremity, an excess
ready to prune, ready to sprout or split. Mitosis
making a daughter to offer to the spoils
of this world, evil as the emerald politics
of an angry man, a misogynist man, animate orange
head of a man filling up my media screens.
It's enough to keep me awake, though I am already
sleepless in my state. Salt of earth, of what I eat,
sweats through my fervent skin on nights
I toss and turn. Not more food, nor tea and milk,
nor rubbing my clitoris to climax
will calm this restless vessel.

I am marked. I am one becoming two, becoming one
again, and then the fortune of three—the opposite sex
(the father), the baby, and back to me. I am branded
by my sex, which reproduces for you, becomes a creature
betrayed for you. And for me, my body deceives me. Stretches
and aches and jabs at me. My own expanding flesh
leers at me, a hinky afterthought, like the afterbirth
that will tug its way out after the wanted thing.

False Labor at 26 Weeks

9:20 pm
tightness in
abdomen when
got up to pee

heartburn feeling
and nauseous

lower back
and hips
hurt

rectum pressure,
no poop

Ate bowl of cereal,
more pee
back in bed at
9:30 pm

10:04 pm
tightness in
abdomen when
got up to pee

drank more water
ate Tums
lay down,
no more tightness

10:35 pm
tightness in
abdomen when
got up to pee

6:40 am
tightness in
abdomen while
lying down

went away when
got up to pee

1:39 pm
tightening while
sitting / reclining
on the couch

1:48 pm
tightness when
I stood up to go
upstairs
to lie down
in bed

1:58 pm
tightness lying
on left side

drank a glass of H_2O

2:30 pm
tightness
got up to pee
drank water

2:39 pm
tightness
sitting up
pee, BM, soft

3:11 pm
tightness and
pelvic pressure

6:20 pm
tightness

6:29 pm
tight

6:38 pm
hospital

Feel the Fibroid

Feel the fibroid
      hard as plastic
            inside you.

Wish for it to soften,
          to disappear.

Why can't it do this
      when you've perfected
          the act?

Does my disappearance
      create the void
          it fills?

If I come back,
          will it go away?

How is there room
      for both of us
          in this body?

I have filled myself
      with baby. Must you,
          fibroid,

occupy the same space?
      Was my uterus empty
          too long?

My womb is not for rent.
    You're squatting and I'm
        an angry landlord.

I'd like to evict you.
    Change the locks,
        board up the doors.

Kick

    you

        out.

I want the unfurling of my baby girl.
    It's she I want to cradle
        when I place my hands below my belly button.

I want to love everything:
    the lone crow's cry out my window
        and the quiet growing human inside me.

I want to love my body again.
    Watch me do this magic trick.
        Fibroid, you tough bastard, I'm through.

The Missing Poem: Birth

urgent   :
                        you arrived
           seven pounds,
                        thirteen and a half ounces

                                   unfed
pink daughter

           father's forearms

preeclampsia   swollen

              fibroid
              my uterus
              you grew

around

                        frantic

           moments,

cry,   you didn't

three days   squeaked, like a
           world   so many doctors
rush   .   .   in

              I hemorrhaged
                        up inside
           before the cervix closed

                              yelled
            feel guilty

                        labor

"Let it go."
                  me

                  birth force
                                    go—let you
go   swooped
                  stridor baby
striped blanket

still   I swooned

Breastfeeding Dyad

your shoulder is a star

        shooting its way into

the gravitational pull of me

        your mouth, a black hole

sucking what light I make

        into the core of you

oh, these worlds we are now

        you and I

tied together

        like a planet and moon

A(u)reola

There is a world at my fingertips. Or,
I am the world—fingertipped. Or, she is:
She grips me with the tips of her fingers.

She is my world. Or, I am hers;
I touch her with the tips of my fingers.
She suckles the round planet that is my breast.
Her fingers curl around her own palm and form a fist.
She is a world grabber, world eater, and I am that world. Or,

I am the sun, giving life to her, the planet, the world. No,
I am the world. And she, my moon and stars.
She orbits around the nippled globe of me.
Makes visible the milk-white halo.

Birth of a Daughter

I birth myself anew
as I birth you, daughter.

I am me plus and minus the cells expunged
to create you, daughter.

You arrive, doll-sized, bright-eyed, a sponge
soaking up my milk—

more cells I shed to make you, feed you,
daughter. Am I the mushroom—

*the fleshy, spore-bearing fruiting body
of a fungus,* or are you? Or do we

form one as a verb? Do we mushroom
into this life, together, daughter?

I write this as you are away; we call it school,
though it is June and you are three.

I work, I write, I sit outside
in the sun, and I can't lie: it's delicious,

this time away from you;
it's precious, as are you.

It has only taken me 42 years to realize
I am precious, too.

Write Like a Fighter

Write like a fighter. In bursts of adrenaline. Kicked down and jumping back up at the buzzer, which is now the sound of your child, waking up in the middle of the night—2:08 a.m. to be exact—and this time simply stating, clear as a fighter bell: "Mommy!"

You fight the sleep and go to her. Pick her up off the futon on the floor and snuzzle her pink neck. She giggles. There are worse things going on at 2:08 in the morning. You cradle her and unsheathe your boob from the secret black folds of your nursing hoodie. She grabs on like a leech. Her free hand wanders all over your body—which is no longer yours. Up and through the opening of your sweatshirt, up to your neck, back down to your breast. She explores your flesh and kneads it like a cat. And although there are no claws, this bothers you. You keep nursing anyway. You kiss her forehead. You marvel at the porcelain smoothness of her face. You pray for sleep, which you are fighting in order to do this: giving yourself over to her. You think how much she takes from you. Your time. Your bodily fluids. Half your DNA. Your sleep. Oh, how much sleep's been stolen in two years' time.

She suckles you until you are sore. Until you're sure there's nothing left. Until the searing pain in your nipple gets stronger. That's ok. You're strong. You're a fighter. You remember giving birth. You can do anything. Ow. The nipple and the wandering pinching grasps of her hands. You insert your finger between her mouth and your areola. Relief.

"Baba," she says. You hand her the bottle that sits in wait next to her bed. She takes it. Relief again. Maybe she'll fall back asleep. She gulps and sputters and pops the bottle out of her mouth.

"All done," she says, and it's the first time she says it correctly, pronouncing each letter, even the "n" in "done." Prior to this moment, she would say, "All dah." This is a milestone, you note, and tuck it away in your brain. You fought sleep and pain to bear witness to this: your daughter's evolution of language. You note how proud you are, as if you had something to do with her programmed continuum of development. As if her brain wasn't wired for language, with or without you. Meanwhile, your brain's been rewired for insomnia. What's the point of falling asleep when any minute you're going to be slapped awake by the cries of your child?

She does not go to sleep after the baba. She asks for the other side, which sounds like "Guh guys." It's the funniest thing she says, and now you and your husband have an inside joke. You think of your breasts as Italian mobsters. That's ok. Sex is a distant memory. The stuff of dreams. Dreams you've been two-stepping as you fight this sleep monster.

After the other side and the baby's breath getting slower and slower and the amazing miracle of another human being falling asleep in your arms—the trust!—you kiss her so many times you lose count. You drape a million blankets over her side-sleeping body. You sneak out of her room and walk straight past your own bed, and go downstairs because now you're hungry. And you grab your book to keep you company while you snack silently in your quiet kitchen. And you notice the bookmark-slash-business card that falls out of your book and onto the floor. It reads: "Fight like a writer." You think, *Fight like a writer? ha! What about write like a fighter?* And you grab your journal, and you do.

My Toddler's Scrambled Eggs

sit cold and yellow, gelatinous now, on the kitchen island where
    she has her own spot: a wooden learning tower pushed
    against the side where she can climb up and down, stand to
    eat, paint, or play.

Mostly we eat here, together, at the island. She and I. Me and her.

Let's be honest, usually I don't eat; I watch her. And maybe eat her
    leftovers. But not this time. Who likes cold scrambled
    eggs? Why did I even leave them here, paper plate and all?

Am I lazy, today? Tired? Bored? Sure. All three. It's almost one
    o'clock; I'm in my pajamas, so is she. I haven't even
    brushed my teeth.

What do I want with the outside world anyway? The rain outside
    a constant drizzle—soft, light, cold, bitter. We could stay
    in, mother and daughter, cocooned in light and nursery
    rhymes all day.

Only one will emerge—changed, grown, with new language
    acquired. The other (ok it's me) will not emerge at all,
    but will remain—like the eggs—untouched; a soggy
    memory.

Heart Healthy

My mother loved pistachios. She would sit at the kitchen table
with a plastic bagful, crack them open dutifully, one by one with
her teeth so as not to ruin her painted nails, pile a hefty mound of
empty shells on the glass tabletop. Brown papery skins would
escape and skitter at too deep breaths, from her every sigh.

> I should have known, this is why
> my daughter now eats pistachios so fervidly

and full of heart. My mother loved other foods, too: matzo brei, the
fried egg, onion powder and matzo crumbled into a bowl of egg
whisked with a fork—I made this my own, but not her veal and
chicken cutlets fried in Crisco, the sizzling sound of meat crackling
in fake lard—that pop, like the popping crack of pistachios.

> "More. Nut," my daughter demands
> her chubby finger pointing to the bag

lined with the words *Wonderful Pistachios ... heart healthy ...
scientific evidence ... heart disease ... reduce the risk* (risk: the
possibility of loss or injury; peril). My mother, inhaling bags of
pistachios, a box of Devil's Food cake, Devil Dogs, Entenmann's
chocolate frosted donuts, whose black lacquer cracked when you
took a big, healthy bite. My mother, the dark bedroom. My mother,
the bedridden muffles, unfit words from her heart: "Get out."
"Leave me alone." "I wish you were never born."

> This early morning
> my toddler watches me pry open

the shell, snap the nut in half, making it fit for her to eat. Did you know that pistachios cause migraines? That most nuts do? My mother's migraines took her over; made her nuts. Each cracked nut, each box of Entenmann's, little loaded weapons upon her body. My mother was 69 when she died, of so many broken parts; mostly her heart. Her name, Linda, was a song. My daughter, now two—Saskia—is a mouthful.

> "Pi-stash-ee-oh," I say, placing each halved nut
> in front of her, eschewing
> a tiny death. I watch my daughter—or is it
> my mother—chew and chew.

The Girl is Three

The girl is three and my husband and I talk about buying a gun
to keep us safe when the fascists come.

The girl is three and we talk about selling the house, buying an RV,
traveling the country.

I worry, to where could we travel that is safe?
Where the radicals and snowflakes don't chafe?

The girl is three and already white men want to control her ovaries
in many states except for the one in which we live. Why leave?

The girl is three, and we cannot leave her.
She will need us in this world for far

too long. See, just now she runs up to me: "Mommy?!"
"Can you put this on cozy, fuzzy, bear eye?"

I am needed to put a doll-sized, cloth pair of glasses
on the eyes of a stuffed bear wearing a red cap and gown. Task

done, the three-year-old runs off, grabs her keyboard,
and sings "E-I-E-I-O!"

See? I have important work to do. I am fine-motor-skill-finisher.
I am witness. I am mother.

And the girl, is only three—sitting,
naked legs wide open—singing.

What Feral Means to a Writing Mom

"there's a feral / glint in some eyes around here."
—Bill Abbott

Red-faced, dirt-
rimmed sticky-
handed toddler
whining for her
Mommy who
hides upstairs in
her bedroom
to write a poem.
This is the definition
of ferality. No wild
animal but the one
I made and birthed,
hide from now.

7-Minute Fairytale

Oh my, three years old and how can I protect her from the horrors of the world from the trafficking and the cages and the gang rape frat boys in college, will she even make it that far, this is what I think about when I caress her dimply skin, when I hold her in the rocking chair, which she is too big for now but holy cow time moves too fast not like the soft squeaky sway of this wooden rocking chair, the one I bought on Craigslist from a lady who said she raised her two daughters in that chair—rocked and nursed and rocked some more. Are they safe now? I want to ask her. Did they make it through unscathed? And by *they* I mean their bodies, of course, girls and women as only a body, as only how our culture sees them—us—with the vultures swooping down among the most vulnerable bodies, the ones with holes, the pink ones, the moist ones, the soft ones, baby-fat and chubby cheeks, chubbier thighs, at three these are adorable, delectable, delicious, but somewhere someone other than me, her mother, wants to eat her too, gobble her up like the wolf did to Granny, just waiting for the juicier, tastier, red-hooded body of a young girl.

How to Celebrate a Dead Mom's Birthday

Go to Lieutenant Island on Cape Cod with your family:
your husband, your father-in-law, your son and your daughter.

Hear the tides of history in your husband's voice
when he tells you, *this place is special.*

When you get there, fly a kite.
In the absence of sun, notice how the sky

is a washed-out version of the color of the sea.
Go for a walk with your teenage son; hear

laughter on the ghost of wind even though
you are the only two humans in sight. Maybe it's not laughter

but the seagull's cry. Watch the birds take flight.
Walk back. Relinquish your journal to the toddler who

imitates you by filling pages with black,
inky, squiggles. Take pictures of her

with your phone. Post them on Facebook with a blue
heart emoji. Say, this daughter is so very Susan.

Say, in your head, how much you miss her. Don't
cry. Especially in front of your husband, her son.

To My Daughter Sleeping Soundly in the Middle of the Night

You are the reason the world
    keeps turning,

the reason people like me
    do anything at all.

You are the reason we want
    no wars.

You are the one perfect existence
    to an imperfect earth.

One touch of your cheek
    makes angels cry.

Notes

"A(u)reola" is a mashup title of these two homophonous words:
> Areola: noun: a small circular area, in particular the ring of pigmented skin surrounding a nipple.
> Aureole: noun [Also au·re·o·la]: a radiance surrounding the head or the whole figure in the representation of a sacred personage; any encircling ring of light or color; halo.

"Birth of a Daughter" references the Wikipedia definition for mushroom (en.wikipedia.org/wiki/Mushroom).

"Heart Healthy" references the Merriam-Webster definition for the word risk.

"I Am Marked" was written for *Contemporary Verse 2's* 2016 2-Day Poem Contest, utilizing ten words they provided.

"Write like a Fighter" references the business card quote "Fight like a writer" by Chelsea Clammer, author of *Circadian* (Red Hen, 2017), which I was reading at the time I wrote this piece.

About the Author

Samantha Kolber has received a Ruth Stone Poetry Prize and a Vermont Poetry Society prize, and her manuscript "Jewel Tones" was a semifinalist with the Crab Orchard Series in Poetry's 2019 First Book Prize. She received her MFA from Goddard College and completed post-grad work at Pine Manor College's Solstice MFA Program. Originally from New Jersey, she lives in Montpelier, Vermont, where she coordinates events and marketing for Bear Pond Books and is the Poetry Series Editor at Rootstock Publishing. You can find her poems in many journals, anthologies, and online. Listen to select poems, including "Birth of a Daughter," at her website, samanthakolber.com.

Made in the USA
Middletown, DE
31 August 2020